GEOGRAPHY AND COMMUNITY IN NEW YORK CITY

NANCY HICER

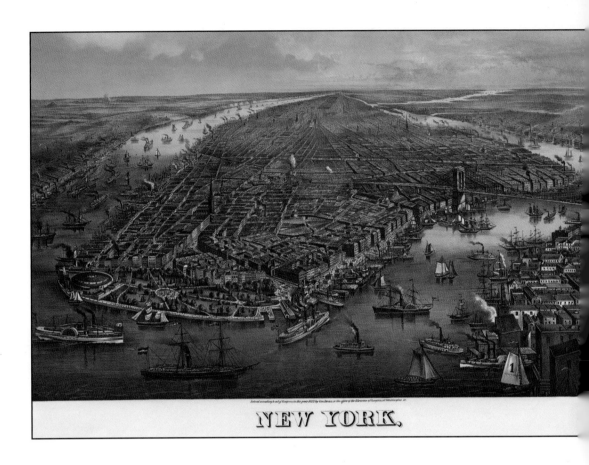

NEW YORK,

Communities are groups of people who choose to live together. Geography describes what the land is like: its hills, rivers, and islands, for example. A community often grows in a place because of its specia**location**.

2

ommunities grow for many reasons.

ometimes people who have the same

ofession want to be near each other in a

ecial location.

In the 1600s, Turtle Bay in Manhattan gave **shelter** to ships from the bad weather of the East River. This area became an important place for shipbuilding. Many boatbuilders came to live here.

1645, Dutch **settlers** came to live near
ushing Creek in what is now Flushing,
ueens. This was a beautiful area of forests.
ter, the first **businesses** in North America
at grew trees for sale started here. Kissena
rk still has many special trees from this time.

The Fulton Fish Market opened in 1822 at Fulton Street and the East River in Manhatta This special location made it easy for fishing boats to come here to sell their fish. A community of **fishermen**, fish sellers, and fis restaurants grew here. This community is nc in the Bronx.

ometimes people who come from the same

ountry want to live together in the same

ecial location. Sometimes the place they

noose reminds them of their home country.

Staten Island has many trees, hills, and **harbors**. It sits in New York Bay. People from many different countries choose to live on Staten Island.

metimes people who share the same

story want to form a community together.

ey choose to live in an area where they

n help each other.

The Dutch and English settlers in New York City found the land of Brooklyn excellent for growing food. Later farmers sold the land to people who wanted to build homes. James Weeks, a free African American, bought a home in 1838 in what is now Weeksville in Crown Heights, Brooklyn.

metimes communities decide to change

geography of a place near them to

ake it better. Orchard Beach in the Bronx

s made to give the people of New York a

autiful, long beach on Long Island Sound.

Glossary

businesses: companies that sell things

fishermen: people who fish

harbors: safe bodies of water deep enough for ships to rest

location: place

profession: a job that needs a special education and skill

settlers: people who go to live in a new place where there are few or no people

shelter: a place that protects people and things